A fishing village turn
popularly known as '
country unveils her s
ternational screens, b   .o
meet with feet in thei   ....size is an endless trove of
upscale novelties and sentimental keepsakes, and an infinite heart
that fuels even the boldest of pursuits. With a kindred community
and tenacious people, this minuscule red dot has been put on the
world map as an experimental ground that creatives from all over
the world can call home.

CITIx60: Singapore explores the tropical island nation in five aspects,
covering architecture, art spaces, shops and markets, eating and
entertainments. With expert advice from 60 stars of Singapore's
creative scene, this book guides you to the real attractions of the
city-state for an authentic taste of Singapore life.

Contents

Before You Go

BASIC INFO

Currency
Singaporean Dollar (SGD/S$)
US$1: S$1.4

Time zone
GMT +8

Singapore does not observe DST

Dialling
International calling: +65

Weather (average range)
Daily temperature: 25–33°C / 77–91°F

Singapore has no distinctive seasons. Expect hot and humid weather year round, and swift downpours followed by clear skies most days.

USEFUL WEBSITES

Public transport services & journey planner
gothere.sg
smrt.com.sg

EMERGENCY CALLS

Ambulance and fire
995

Police
999

Embassies and high commissions
Australia	+65 6836 4100
China	+65 6471 2117
Indonesia	+65 6737 7422
Japan	+65 6235 8855
S. Korea	+65 6256 1188
U.K.	+65 6424 4200
U.S.	+65 6476 9100

AIRPORT EXPRESS TRANSFER

Changi Airport (CG2) <-> City (taxi)
Journey: ~30 mins
One-way: S$20–40 (metered)
Surcharge for all trips originating from the airport: S$3 or S$5 (F–Su: 1700–0000)

PUBLIC TRANSPORT IN SINGAPORE

Subway (MRT)
Boat
Bus
Taxi*

Means of Payment
Cash
ezLink card

Taxi fares are metered. Surcharges will be added during the small hours (50% of metered fare, 0000–0600 daily), rush hours (25% of metered fare, M–F: 0600–0930, daily: 1800–0000) and for rides starting from Central Business areas (S$3)

PUBLIC HOLIDAYS

January	1 New Year's Day, Chinese New Year (or in February)*
March/April	Good Friday*
May	1 Labour Day, Vesak Day*
July	Hari Raya Puasa*
August	9 National Day
September	Hari Raya Haji*
October	Deepavali*
December	25 Christmas Day

Holidays* observe their respective calendars and vary by year. If a holiday falls on a Sunday, the closest weekday after becomes a 'substitute' day. Museums, galleries and shops are likely to be closed or operate on special hours around Christmas and New Year's Day.

FESTIVALS / EVENTS

January
Singapore Art Week
www.artweek.sg
Artstage
www.artstage.com

March
Singapore Design Week & Singaplural
designsingapore.org/SDW

June
Baybeats
www.esplanade.com/baybeats
The O.P.E.N. (through July)
www.sifa.sg/theopen
Ultra Singapore
ultrasingapore.com

August
Singapore Night Festival
nightfest.sg

September
A Design Film Festival
FB: A Design Film Festival
Archifest (through October)
archifest.sg

October
Singapore Fashion Week
singaporefashionweek.com.sg
Illustration Arts Festival
illustrationartsfest.org
Singapore International Photography Festival
sipf.sg

November
Neon Lights
www.neonlights.sg
Singapore International Film Festival
sgiff.com

December
ZoukOut
zoukout.com

Event days vary by year. Please check for updates online.

UNUSUAL OUTINGS

Audio art tours
voicemap.me/tour/singapore

City tour guided by site-specific art
ohopenhouse.org

Free architecture walks
www.archiwalks.com

Be an urban farmer for a day
Open Farm Community (#42)

Themed trails & stories behind places
www.locomole.com

SMARTPHONE APPS

Transport services & journey planner
SG BusLeh, Citymapper

Taxi booking service with driver tracker
Grab

Restaurant directory & reviews
Burpple

REGULAR EXPENSES

Kopi
S$1

Domestic / international mail (postcards)
S$0.40/S$0.60

Gratuities
Diners: optional on top of 10% service charge
Hotels: S$2@bag for porter
Licensed taxis: round up the fare to the nearest S$1

Goods & Services Tax (GST)
7% on most purchases, refundable at Singapore airports or cruise terminals within two months of purchases over S$100.

Count to 10

What makes Singapore so special?

Illustrations by Guillaume Kashima aka Funny Fun

The success story of Southeast Asia began with four ethnicities, but this melting pot of cultures only grew more effervescent as friends from across the globe arrived with their stories. Singapore has become a vivid tapestry of cultures, stitched together by eclectic influences lent to her architecture, food, arts and lifestyles. Whether you're here for a day or a week, see what Singapore's creative class considers an essential to-do list.

GARDENS BY THE BAY

1

Architecture

People's Park Complex & Golden Mile Complex (#6)
by DP Architects

The Interlace
by Ole Scheeren, RSP Architects Planners & Engineers

Blessed Sacrament Church (#11)
by Y. Gordon Dowsett of Iversen, van Sitteren & Partners

National Gallery Singapore (#13)
by studioMilou, CPG Consultants

Henderson Waves @The Southern Ridges
by IJP Corporation, RSP Architects Planners & Engineers

Esplanade
by Michael Wilford & Partners, Russell Johnson & DP Architects

Gardens by the Bay (#4)
by Grant Associates, Wilkinson Eyre Architects

2

Dimensional
City Views

Lepark (#59)

Skybridge
50/F, The Pinnacle@Duxton
(0900–2100 daily)
pinnacleduxton.com.sg

Singapore Sports Hub
www.sportshub.com.sg

Potong Pasir river bank

ION Sky
www.ionorchard.com

SuperTree by IndoChine
indochine-group.com

Merlion Park
One Fullerton

Faber Peak Singapore
www.faberpeaksingapore.com

3

Staple Food
(Spicy)

Nyonya Laksa
Sungei Road Laksa (charcoal-fired)
sungeiroadlaksa.com.sg

Otah (grilled fishcake)
Lee Wee & Brother's Foodstuff
leeweebrothers.com

Chilli Crab
Mellben Seafood, *melben.com.sg*

Curry & Roti Prata
Mr and Mrs Mohgan's
Super Crispy Roti Prata
7 Crane Rd., 429356

South Indian Thali & Appam
Madras New Woodlands Restaurant
14 Upper Dickson Rd., 207474

Bak Kut Teh (spiced pork ribs soup)
Founder, *347 Balestier Rd., 329777*

**Mee Siam (rice vermicelli in a light,
spicy, sweet & sour gravy)**
Famous Sungei Road Trishaw Laksa
@Hong Lim Market & Food Centre

4

Staple Food
(Mild)

Traditional breakfast
Chin Mee Chin Confectionery (#44),
Tong Ah Eating House

Chicken Rice
Heng Ji @Chinatown Complex Market

Popiah (Fujian-style fresh rolls)
Yue Yi Tai Shan Popiah, *Clementi*

**Nasi Padang
(rice with Indonesian specialties)**
Warong Nasi, *pariaman.com.sg*

Lor Mee (braised noodles)
Zhong Xing Foo Chow Fishballs
148 Silat Ave., 160148

Tutu Kueh (coconut cake)
Tan's Tu Tu Coconut Cake
22B Havelock Rd., 162022

Tau Huay (soft bean curd)
Selegie Soya Bean
1002 Upper Serangoon Rd., 534734

5

Top Hawker Fare & Street Food

Sambal Stingray, Rojak, Satay Bee Hoon (rice vermicelli), Sugarcane Juice, Chai Tow Kway (fried carrot cake)
Chomp Chomp Food Centre, East Coast Lagoon Food Village (#46)

Varied Chinese & local specialties
Tiong Bahru Market, *tiongbahru.market*

Indian food haven
Tekka Market (#31)

Xin Mei Xiang Lor Mee & Roast Paradise
Old Airport Road Food Centre

Semi-authentic open space
Newton Circus, Gluttons Bay

Famous stalls, with air-conditioning
Food Republic

Authentically local
Hong Lim Market & Food Centre

6

Art & Original Designs

Local novelty gifts
Supermama (#34)
Naiise, *naiise.com*

Specialised bookstores
Kinokuniya, Basheer (#36)

Workshops & exhibitions curated by kinetic
K+ Curatorial Space (#21)

Paper & print work exhibitions
Tyler Print Institute, *stpi.com.sg*

Homegrown fashion & designs
Rockstar, *rockstar.com.sg*
National Design Centre
www.designsingapore.org/ndc

Photography-focused Art Space
DECK (#22)

Asian homeware
SCENE SHANG, *sceneshang.com*
Gallery & Co., *galleryand.co*

7

Markets

Quarterly farmers' market
Kranji Countryside
kranjicountryside.com

Designer items, live shows & food
The Local People
thelocalpeoplesg.com

A modern take on food & groceries
PasarBella@TheGrandstand
pasarbella.com

By Red Dot Design Museum
MAAD (#23)

Weekend flea market for local designs & crafts
Public Garden, *public-garden.com*

Retro toys & action figures
China Square Central (#25)

Everything for free
Singapore Really Really Free Market
FB: SRRFM)

8

Edible Mementos

Shermay's Cilicuka Sauce
www.shermay.com

Chicken Rice Chilli Sauce
Boon Tong Kee
boontongkee.com.sg

Sauce kits & noodles
Prima Taste
www.primataste.com.sg

Tropical fruit marmalade
Straits Preserves
straitspreserves.com

Pandan chiffon & pineapple tarts
Bengawan Solo
bengawansolo.com.sg

Kaya swiss roll
Rich and Good Cake Shop
24 Kandahar St., 198887

Kaya
Ya Kun Kaya Toast
www.yakun.com

9

Indie Music

Gallery, craft beer, alternative music
Kult Café, kultkafe.com

Largest local gig database, artist interviews & gig listing
bandwagon, bandwagon.sg

Creative collective, show host & music label
DUNCE., FB: iamadunce

Underground music collective & show host
Syndicate, www.syndicate.sg

Monthly open-format nights
Good Times @Blu Jaz Cafe (#58)

Art Space by day, full-on nightclub by night
Canvas, FB: Canvas Club

Local releases
Curated Records (#33),
Cat Socrates, Roxy Records & Trading,
Hear Records

10

Closer to Nature

Watch red junglefowl
Fort Canning Park

Seek saltwater crocodiles
Sungei Buloh Nature Park

Hike around Chek Jawa Wetlands
Pulau Ubin

Listen to the sounds of tropical forests
Mount Faber, Bukit Timah Hill,
MacRitchie Reservoir Park

Otters sighting
Punggol Waterway Park

Nature park created from a disused granite quarry
Bukit Batok Town Park
aka Little Guilin

Unspoilt powdery beaches
Lazarus Island

Icon Index

 Opening hours   Admission

 Address   Facebook

 Contact   Website

Remarks

 Scan QR codes to access Google Maps and discover the area around each destination. Internet connection required.

60x60

60 Local Creatives x 60 Hotspots

From vast cityscapes to the tiniest glimpses of everyday exchanges, there's always something to provoke your imagination. 60X60 points you to 60 haunts where 60 arbiters of taste cut their teeth.

Landmarks & Architecture   SPOTS · 01 – 12

Beyond the iconic Marina Bay Sands skyline, the landscape abounds with futuristic designs, pockets of history, and residential districts that overflow with character.

Cultural & Art Spaces   SPOTS · 13 – 24

With a medley of the polished, nostalgic and quirky, 24 hours are barely enough to immerse in the prized museums and unconventional art spaces that Singapore has to offer.

Markets & Shops   SPOTS · 25 – 36

There is more to this shopping wonderland than international brands. Living up to its title is an array of fascinating turfs, underrated hotspots for thrifting and vibrant pop-ups.

Restaurants & Cafés   SPOTS · 37 – 48

Much of her culinary heritage can be traced in hawker centres, but these are only a subset of a food scene spruced up with hip establishments and inventive stunts.

Nightlife   SPOTS · 49 – 60

In the land of eternal summer, every night gives exactly 12 hours to be partied away on classy rooftops and imaginative bars, or buzzing 24-hour spots in the locals' hood.

Landmarks & Architecture

Flashy skyscrapers, heritage buildings and rustic heartlands

Singapore's time as a British colony perfectly explains the curious contrast between Art Deco masterpieces like Parkview Square (#1) and Brutalist buildings like Golden Mile Complex (#6). But she has a multi-religious society to thank for a landscape on which futurism intertwines with multiple facets of her people's history.

Only in Singapore will you find Sri Mariamman Temple (*244 South Bridge Rd., 058793*), an intricate Hindu temple right smacked in the middle of Chinatown, and realise it is just the first of many surprises. A nostalgic trail of dowdy five-foot ways would later lead you to The Pinnacle@Duxton (*1 Cantonment Rd., 080001*), where 50 storeys of award-clinching modernity is juxtaposed against all of history itself.

The 1980s linger in faded walls and animal-shaped playgrounds at Toa Payoh and Dakota – the country's oldest public housing estates developed by Housing and Development Board (HDB). In these columns that over 80 percent of Singaporeans dwell in, diversity is found between the rice sacks of Indian "mama shops" (sundry stores) and the flames of incense burners during the Chinese Hungry Ghost Festival.

Darius Ou
Graphic designer

Born in 1993, Darius Ou is a native Singaporean specialising in branding and graphic design.

PARKROYAL on Pickering P.015

Chan Ee Mun
Senior associate, WOHA

A practicing architect, Chan Ee Mun is an experience seeker who works to shape experiences. He can mostly be found in coffee corners (the local variety) around Singapore.

Dawn Ng
Visual artist

With a background in studio art and journalism, Dawn Ng has been straddling art, design and advertising for ten years, working with mediums such as collage, light and installation.

Parkview Square P.014

Hyderabad Road P.016

Jovian Lim
Photographer

An early riser, Jovian Lim love the clean breakfast and tranquillity each morning brings. He intends to work like a painter, exploring the space between human and the sublime.

Pearl Bank Apartments P.020

Michelle Lin
Founder, The Strangely Good

The Strangely Good thrives on brand new perspectives to deliver idea. Their broad range of competencies and interests in different disciplines drives their all-round and distinct approach.

Joshua Comaroff & Ong Ker Shing, *Lekker Architects*

After studying architecture and landscape at Harvard, the two started to cooperate as Lekker in 2002. The duo generally enjoys working on things that are small, and close to home.

Gardens by the Bay P.017

Golden Mile Complex P.022

Melvin Ong
Industrial designer

Vastly inspired by nature, Melvin Ong creates his crafts under the name Desinere. His designs are a reflection of his experiences and thoughts.

Mojoko
Creative director, Kult Magazine

Mojoko aka Steve Lawler makes art, directs *Kult Magazine* and curates for Kult Gallery. His works have been showcased in independent galleries worldwide.

Chang Yong Ter
Founder, CHANG Architects

Chang Yong Ter holds that architecture is a work from the mind and heart. Part of his design process involves unlearning, forgetting, and self-discoveries of the basics and origin.

Yu Yah Leng
Owner, Foreign Policy Design

Creatively driven, Yu Yah Leng is a creative director, idea maker and problem solver who co-runs Foreign Policy with Arthur Chin. Together they craft, realise and build brands.

Pann Lim
Co-founder, Kinetic

I co-founded and creatively direct Kinetic and K+ Curatorial Space. I love design, advertising, art, music, movies, photography, furniture and anything related to visual culture.

Hanyi Lee
CCO, The Secret Little Agency

I lead a band of misfits at The Secret Little Agency, a creative agency headquartered in Singapore.

1 Parkview Square
Map I, P.108

Completed in 2002, this Art Deco-style office tower has little to do with Bruce Wayne's home city, but its resemblance to New York City's Chanin building has given it the nickname 'Gotham Building'. Adorned with rich hand-crafted detailing and brown granite on the outside, the structure houses the Embassies of Austria, Mongolia and the UAE, and an impressive bar that boasts a three-storey wine chiller in its lobby area. A stroll in the courtyard will lead you to the bronze effigies of Shakespeare and Chopin among other historical figures.

🏠 *600 North Bridge Rd., 188778*
URL *www.parkviewsquare.com*

"No other place in Singapore will you find such a beautiful Art Deco-style building."

– Darius Ou

2 PARKROYAL on Pickering
Map C, P.105

Awarded for its plentiful energy-saving and nature-inspired features, this gorgeous part-forest, part-hotel mutant has even earned itself a cameo in Aleksander Bach's *Hitman: Agent 47* (2015). Designed by WOHA architects as an extension of the nearby Hong Lim Park, PARKROYAL on Pickering's silhouette is punctuated with trees, mimicry of rock formations, and crisp foliage hanging from room balconies. When it rains, water collected from the towering terraces trickle down to irrigate planters on the lower floors.

🏠 *3 Upper Pickering St., 058289*
📞 *+65 6809 8888*
📘 *PARKROYAL on Pickering Hotel, Singapore*

"Sip a drink in one of the overhanging birdcages suspended 25 metres above the streets and enjoy panoramic views of the city."

– Chan Ee Mun, WOHA

3 Hyderabad Road
Map P, P.110

Slipping under the radar of royalty streets is Hyderabad Road, a meandering fringe of Hort Park named after the last Nizam, or Indian Prince, who owned properties here. What used to be British military grounds remains a fairly uncharted territory of Alexandra today, dotted with colonial profiles, like a beautiful 1930s campus (S P Jain School Of Global Management) and an intimate French-Italian restaurant nestled in lush greenery. Its former identity was never entirely erased, and you can still see mounds of earth that conceal underground bunkers within.

🏠 *Hyderabad Rd., 119578*

"In a city that never stops changing, time seems to stand still among the sprawl of old and beautiful colonial houses."

– Dawn Ng

④ Gardens by the Bay
Map M, P.109

Avatar was the first blockbuster to revolutionise 3D films, but the set pretty much comes alive in 4D at Gardens by the Bay, an otherworldly garden that will give film director James Cameron a run for his money. The eco-friendly horticultural-themed attraction has a 23°C Flower Dome that showcases ever-changing blooms like cherry blossoms and tulips, and an aerial walkway at the Supertree Grove for unreal strolls. Stay after dusk to witness a kaleidoscopic spectacle of illuminated Supertrees. You decide if this is a garden within a city or vice versa.

🕐💲 Daily, 0900-2100: Conservatories, $28/15, Skyway: $8/5; 0500-0200: Outdoor Gardens
🏠 18 Marina Gardens Dr., 018953   📞 +65 6420 6848
URL www.gardensbythebay.com.sg

"There are lockers and water coolers around, so you don't have to carry your bag around; thoughtful!"

– Jovian Lim

5 Pearl Bank Apartments
Map C, P.105

For four decades now, Pearl Bank Apartments by native architect Tan Cheng Siong has been Outram's housing icon and a magnet for lingering gazes and inquisitive *oohs* and *aahs*. Oriented to minimise solar heat gain and maximise views, the horseshoe tower offers three types of split-level apartments to 1,500 inhabitants, making it one of Singapore's densest high-rise experiments in the 1970s. As one of the oldest buildings around, the condo has fought valiantly against the common fate of its kind – en-bloc sales and demolition – for conservation status to stick around.

🏠 *1 Pearl Bank, 169016*

"Take lift B up to the 37th floor and down the stairway for a vertigo, inducing yet scenic trip down and a good view of the PSA terminal and Chinatown."

– Michelle Lin, The Strangely Good

6 Golden Mile Complex
Map I, P.108

The staggered design of Golden Mile Complex is an anomaly in residential architecture, and a spectacular example of Singapore's Brutalist and Metabolist principles. As the first and only segment of a larger planning scheme to ease overcrowding in the 1960s, the project proposed a vertical utopian with shaded flats, shops and offices organised within a 16-storey building. It's now known as Little Thailand for the Thai vendors tucked inside, and the only place in town that celebrates Songkran. Come armed with water blasters in April. There's no missing a splashing good time!

🏠 5001 Beach Rd., 199588
URL www.goldenmilecomplex.sg

"See the building from both sides before exploring the shops inside. The cheap and cheerful Thai food is more abundant here than elsewhere in Singapore."
– Joshua Comaroff & Ong Ker Shing, Lekker Architects

7 The Southern Ridges
Map P, P.110

Those who fancy a picturesque hike sans the rugged terrain will find The Southern Ridges to be an oasis within a concrete gridlock. The 10km trail connects Mount Faber and West Coast, and is strewn with vantage points of the city and the Southern Islands. Sceneries re-shuffle at every turn, from an elevated zigzag walkway through The Forest Walk's canopies to the whimsical curves and arches of Henderson Waves Bridge that LED-illuminates come nightfall. Reflections at Keppel Bay designed by Daniel Libeskind can be spied in the distance, and you'd see why the locals call it Tony Stark's mansion.

🕙 *Lighting hours for Alexandra Arch: 1900–0000 daily, Henderson Waves: –0700 daily*
🏠 *Henderson Rd., Mount Faber Park, 099203*
🔗 *No wheelchair access*

"*The Henderson Waves is quite a remarkable architectural structure where you can enjoy panoramic views of Singapore among treetops.*"
– Melvin Ong, Desinere

023

8 Haw Par Villa
Map N, P.110

Expect no jolly at this theme park, only spine-chilling statues set within a wonderland of oriental pagodas, bridges, and dungeons. You'd imagine the depicted violence to warrant an M18 rating, but it's ironically a routine excursion for schoolchildren. There is beauty in its graphic nature that, while less palatable, stands for a long-forgotten fragment of Chinese culture surrounding folklore and mythology. Intrepid urban explorers can take their pick from *10 Courts Of Hell* to *Journey To The West*. Visit with an open mind and strong heart.

🕑 *0900-1900 daily*
🏠 *262 Pasir Panjang Rd., 118628*

"Bring a camera!"

– Mojoko aka Steve Lawler, Kult Magazine

9 Kampong Lorong Buangkok

Map S, P.111

Before public flats, Singaporeans lived in wooden attap houses and kindred communities divided only by flimsy metal gates. Four decades came and went, but time had come to a standstill in mainland Singapore's last surviving *kampong* (village) since 1956. To over 20 families at Kampong Lorong Buangkok, home looks like pastel zinc roofs and worn picket fences, with the sounds of roaming chickens in the background. Artists flock to this deserted hideout for concept shoots, and others simply to catch a fast-disappearing sight of rural Singapore.

🏠 *Lor Buangkok, 547557*

"Visit soon before it is gone."

– Chang Yong Ter, CHANG Architects

10 Tiong Bahru Estate
Map A, P.104

Ask any locals about Tiong Bahru, millennials will babble on about cafés and bookstores while taxi uncles will fondly recall it as "*gor lau chu*", Hokkien for five-storey house, an origin story long archived in Singapore's oldest housing estate, built by HBD's predecessor in the colonial era. Next to its boxy post-war flats, the 1920s Streamline Moderne Style in Blocks 55-82 contrasts with porthole windows and curved corridors that have been inspired by aerodynamic features. Within this Art Deco mishmash, the last surviving pre-war civilian air raid shelters can be found underneath the U-shaped Block 78 along Guan Chuan Street.

🏠 Tiong Bahru Rd., 160059

"*Look out for the air raid shelter – the last remaining World War II civilian shelter in Singapore.*"

– Yu Yah Leng, Foreign Policy Design

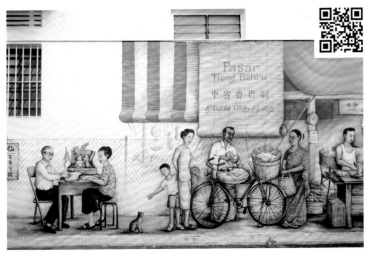

11 Blessed Sacrament Church
Map U, P.111

Ivory, angular structures and classical ornaments are hallmarks of most Catholic church buildings in Singapore but the Blessed Sacrament Church. Metaphorically creating a "tent of meeting", its blue origami-style roof is draped over a traditional parish hall, with exquisite workmanship seeping past its folds and into a symmetrical red brick "attic". Fully appreciate the architect's placement of glass panels in daytime, when sunlight filters into the fairytale's frame through tall ceilings and rainbow grids.

🏠 *1 Commonwealth Dr., 149603*
📞 *+65 6474 0582* 🌐 *www.bsc.org.sg*

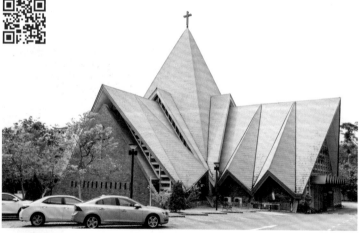

"Once you enter the church, it gives you an unusual tranquillity effect, and that is something I love."
– Pann Lim, Kinetic

12 Singapore Botanic Gardens
Map J, P.109

Fun fact: the illustration on Singapore's five-dollar notes is of a real tree at the gardens. For over two centuries now, the hardy Tembusu has taken root among other heritage trees at the country's first and only UNESCO heritage site. The urban oasis packs plenty of horticultural wonders, be it a lush Ginger Garden or the world's largest display of Singapore's national flower – orchids. Tuck into a wholesome brunch made with local produce at The Halia, or picnic by the Swan Lake and have your mealtime graced by the resident White Mute Swans from Amsterdam.

🕐 0500–0000 daily, Orchid Garden: 0830–1900, Healing Garden: –1930 (W–M & P.H.)
💲 Orchid Garden: $5/1   🏠 1 Cluny Rd., 259569
📞 +65 6471 7138   🔗 www.sbg.org.sg

"As Singapore's only UNESCO World Heritage site, it's a true reflection of what it's like to live in the tropics."

– Hanyi Lee, The Secret Little Agency

Cultural & Art Spaces

Glitzy museums, retrofitted spaces and community projects

Singapore has a penchant for filling old buildings with new life. Alternative films are screened in what was once her largest cinema at The Projector (#19), and contemporary art exhibitions flourish in Gillman Barracks (#24), a former British military camp. In the hearts of this country's sentimental people, 'something old' has a special place.

'Something new' has also sprouted in nightclubs and cafés like Canvas (*canvasvenue.sg*) and Artistry (*www.artistryspace.com*) – with spontaneous displays of artists' work – and even a party of shipping containers–turned–art gallery at DECK (#22). Just around the corner is the Bras Basah and Bugis precinct, best explored during Singapore Night Festival (*nightfest.sg*) when the labyrinth of museums and art spaces comes alive in a nocturnal spectacle.

Not to be missed in the Central Area are the Singapore Art Museum (*www.singaporeartmuseum.sg*) and National Gallery Singapore (#13), a reincarnation of the Supreme Court and City Hall buildings from the 1930s. Especially poignant of stories are told at the National Museum of Singapore (*nationalmuseum.sg*), where the writing desk and clothing of the nation's founding father, Mr. Lee Kuan Yew, are displayed after he passed on in 2015.

Roy Wang Han Yi
Founder, Factory 1611

Trained in fine art since the age of three, Roy Wang art-directs Factory 1611. The studio's specialities include branding, exhibition design, visual communication and fine art.

Lee Kong Chian Natural History Museum
P.036

Tiffany Loy
Industrial designer

Tiffany Loy's work revolves around industrial craft and surface design. She likes to use alternative production methods and exploit existing processes to generate unexpected results.

Justin Zhuang
Co-owner, In Plain Words

Justin Zhuang is a writer and researcher with an interest in design, cities, culture, history and media. Together with Sheere Ng, he manages writing studio In Plain Words.

National Gallery Singapore
P.034

NUS Museum
P.038

Kenny Leck
Co-founder, BooksActually

Kenny Leck co-founded independent bookstore, BooksActually (#29) and helms publishing imprint Math Paper Press. On good sunny days, he sees himself as a 'karung guni' man.

ArtScience Museum
P.040

Jonathan Yuen
Founder, Roots

Jonathan Yuen is the founder and design director of Roots, a multidisciplinary design studio based in Singapore.

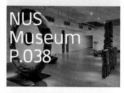

Ernest Goh
Photographer & visual artist

Ernest Goh's work focuses on animals and their relationship with humans. His passion for the nature began as a boy when he could seek fish and spiders at his granny's kampung.

The Substation
P.039

Objectifs
P.041

Nathan Yong
Industrial designer

Nathan Yong acquired his diverse production techniques and crafts at his job as a buyer after graduating school. His work has been approved by President's Design Award in Singapore.

Mulan Gallery
P.044

Adeline Tan
Illustrator & graphic designer

Also known as Mightyellow, Adeline Tan's work tends to be busy and sometimes mildly macabre. She has an imaginary friend called Yellow.

Cherie Ko
Musician

A dabbler in various musical genres, I play guitar for Obedient Wives Club and lead electropop project Pastelpower. I am also the frontwoman of TOMGIRL.

The Projector
P.042

K+ Curatorial Space
P.045

Priscilla Lui & Timo Wong
Founders, Studio Juju

Studio Juju's approach projects fresh and optimistic design visions. Each of their project is a union of simplicity and warmth, functionalism and whimsy, refinement and relevance.

MAAD @Red Dot Design Museum
P.048

Esther Goh
Illustrator & designer

Reality and fiction juxtapose in my work, often characterised by a satirical approach. In my free time, I love to discuss movies, travel and explore forests and trails.

Kelvin Lok
Co-founder, Couple

Couple strives to unfold truths and focus on messages that create memorable and accessible ideas. With that ethos, the graphic design studio has garnered over 28 awards.

DECK
P.046

Gillman Barracks
P.049

13 National Gallery Singapore
Map D, P.106

The pinnacle of Singapore and Southeast Asian modern art is a photogenic reincarnation of the former Supreme Court and City Hall buildings. Rooftop ponds ripple over the City Hall wing's glass ceilings, while over 15,000 aluminium panels cast a gleaming kaleidoscope of lights and shadows by the Supreme Court terrace. Within the gallery, art is tucked into pockets of history. Rotunda dome, formerly a restricted library for lawyers and judges, now opens for viewing alongside two preserved jail cells.

🕐 1000–1900 (Su–Th & P.H.), –2200 (F–Sa & P.H. eve)
💲 $20/15, Local residents admit free
🏠 1 St. Andrew's Rd., 178957
📞 +65 6271 7000 [URL] www.nationalgallery.sg
🔖 Tour schedule varies daily. Booking required.

"This is the perfect place to gain an understanding of the art heritage of Singapore and Southeast Asia, as well as its place and relationship with the world."

– Roy Wang Han Yi, Factory 1611

 14 ## Lee Kong Chian Natural History Museum

Map T, P.111

With enough mammals, plants, amphibians and dinosaur specimens for a sci-fi movie, the museum unveils an uncharted side of the island's history, fronted by three sauropod dinosaur fossils unearthed in Wyoming, US. In the Heritage Gallery, visitors can examine incomplete taxidermy projects and naturalist works founded in the mid-1800s. News on natural science breakthroughs, from the first discovery of a sperm whale in Singapore's waters to the sighting of a critically endangered estuarine crocodile in Serangoon, are also safeguarded here.

🕐 1000–1900 (Tu–Su & P.H.)
💲 $21/13, Local residents: $16/9
🏠 2 Conservatory Dr., National University of Singapore, 117377
📞 +65 6601 3333
URL lkcnhm.nus.edu.sg
🔗 Last admission: 1730

"Be prepared to spend the whole day here! Maybe even two, if you like staring at the beautiful butterflies and bugs."

– Tiffany Loy

15 NUS Museum
Map T, P.111

Over 8,000 pottery, textiles, paintings and
bronzes are nestled in NUS Museum within a
world-class campus. These artefacts date to
as early as the Neolithic times, but their stories
live on in the contours of the Hindu sculptures
and Chinese inscriptions on oracle bones. Off
its main site, Baba House at 157 Neil Road – a
painstakingly restored Peranakan home in
Outram – holds its Straits Chinese collection
in an almost faithful home setting. Its ornate
architecture barely scratches the surface of its
heritage, but you can delve into greater depths
by arranging for a guided tour in advance.

🕐 1000–1800 (Tu–Sa)
🏠 50 Kent Ridge Crsnt., National University of
Singapore, 119279 ☎ +65 6516 8817
🔗 www.nus.edu.sg/museum
🖉 Baba House: by appointment only

"NUS is Singapore's oldest university, which is a nice
place to get lost in."

– Justin Zhuang, In Plain Words

16 The Substation

Map D, P.106

Within the confines of a 1920s shophouse,
Singapore's beacon of contemporary art has
sprouted and grown. The former PUB power
station now owns a black box theatre and a
white cube visual art space, filled mainly with
experimental film, dance, literature and music.
The Substation holds events like First Take and
Secret Screenings, which provide local film-
makers a centre stage, and classes across other
disciplines like photography and playwriting.
The public can look forward to events as varied
as yoga sessions, dialogues, exhibitions and occasional pop-up parties with live gigs.

🕐 *Hours vary with programme*
🏠 45 Armenian St., 179936
📞 +65 6337 7535
URL www.substation.org

"*If Singapore aspires to be anything in the arts
industry, we will always need The Substation.*"

– Kenny Leck, BooksActually

17 ArtScience Museum
Map M, P.109

Where art and design meet science and technology, ArtScience Museum plays host to world-class touring exhibitions, including the Harry Potter film sets and costumes at one point. Its permanent display, Future World, is an immersive digital playground of 16 installations. Look out for Crystal Universe – a captivating display of 170,000 LED lights that fill even adults with childlike wonder whenever its colour changes. True to the museum's overarching synthesis, its structure allows natural light to entre via the "petal tips", and collects rainwater in the centre for reuse.

🕐 1000-1900 daily (admission time: 1000, 1130, 1300, 1430, 1600, 1730)
💲 Combo: $28/24/17 (Booking fee incl.)
🏠 6 Bayfront Ave., 018974   📞 +65 6688 8888
🔗 www.marinabaysands.com/museum

"The museum has been consistently running quality and interesting programmes and exhibitions, and the building itself is a landmark in its own right."

– Jonathan Yuen, Roots

18 Objectifs

Map D, P.106

This canary-yellow building in Bras Basah-Bugis is where you want to wind up at when the chain cineplexes in town are full up. More than an alternative cinematic experience, Objectifs gives enthusiasts a platform to learn from the pros and improve their craft. Hone your scriptwriting and video editing skills at their workshops and seminars, or master the art of shooting architecture by following a street photographer on a field trip. Spare time for treasure digging at Objectifs' shop where underground films, books and art prints by local artists fill the racks.

🕐 1200–1900 (Tu–Sa), –1600 (Su), except P.H.
🏠 155 Middle Rd., 188977 ☎ +65 6336 2957
🔗 www.objectifs.com.sg

"Great exhibitions, good retail store to buy local artwork and great location in the arts district."

– Ernest Goh

19 The Projector

Visiting The Projector is akin to reliving 1970s Singapore. Occupying a foyer of the historic Golden Theatre that has survived the tyranny of development, the independent cinema now screens indie flicks, cult classics and film festival hits in two timeworn but hipster-approved theatres. In the icon of cinematic history, antique charm is preserved on blue bulletins on which movie posters are pinned, and a signage system that uses old-fashioned typography. Both the Green Room and Redrum permit free seating on steep rows of retro flip-up chairs, but pick the latter for enough bean bags to make yourself at home.

🕐 Box office: 1800-2030 (Tu–F), 1300- (Sa–Su & P.H.)
💲 $13.50/11.50
🏠 5/F, Golden Mile Tower, 6001 Beach Rd., 199589
URL theprojector.sg

"No visit is complete without a requisite picture of their iconic spiral staircase on the opposite end of the lobby from the lifts."

– Nathan Yong

20 Mulan Gallery
Map D, P.106

Just shy of a decade old, this small gallery down Armenian Street is surely a fine art collector's dream come true. Be it a temporary exhibition or permanent display, its contents are original in thought and cued by socio-political and cultural influences. Curated collections hail from as far as Europe and as close as home. Standing out from a sea of Spanish sculptors and Chinese photographers is Koh Hong Teng, a local artist whose sentimental paintings speak for the disappearing nuances of HDB living in a rapidly developing city state.

🕐 1130-1830 (Tu-Sa except P.H.)
🏠 36 Armenian St., #01-07, 179934
📞 +65 6738 0810
🔗 www.mulangallery.com.sg

"They support local artists and aim to cultivate and nurture new talents."

– Adeline Tan aka Mightyellow

21 K+ Curatorial Space
Map K, P.109

If a bunch of artists lived under one roof, their hall would look something like K+ Curatorial Space. Touted as the Noah's Ark of local art and design, the 3-in-1 space accommodates a gallery, retail corner and workshop within whitewashed walls and mint green shelves. Something fresh is always brewing, whether it be exhibition concepts or the curated range of homegrown brands they carry. Bazaars and craft classes like sushi roll art and calligraphy are occasionally held at the workshop, where creatives mingle and cross-disciplinary collaborations are sparked.

🕐 1130-2030 (M-Th), 1100- (F-Su & P.H.)
🏠 Scotts Square #03-11/12/13, 6 Scotts Rd., 228209
📞 +65 6694 8896
URL kplus.sg

"The space reinvents itself monthly, showcasing vastly different artists. My pick so far is Japanese whizzkid Mondo, who even came down to do live drawings."

– Cherie Ko

22 DECK

Map D, P.106

DECK was started to make photography accessible for everyone, whether they shot with smartphones or DSLRs. The independent art space takes the shape of 19 shipping containers furnished with ancillary facilities, plonked between LASALLE College of the Arts and NAFA. Check into its galleries and library, where a neat range of photography books and film screenings are available for browsing. Old souls will rejoice at House of Photography, a roving darkroom that revives the forgotten art of analogue photography with courses on film negatives and Polaroid emulsion lifts.

🕐 1200-1900 (Tu-Sa), -1700 (Su),
    except P.H.
🏠 120A Prinsep St., 187937
📞 +65 6734 6578
URL deck.sg

"Steidl's generous donation of more than a thousand titles to DECK founded the basis of the first public library dedicated to photography in Southeast Asia."

– Priscilla Lui & Timo Wong, Studio Juju

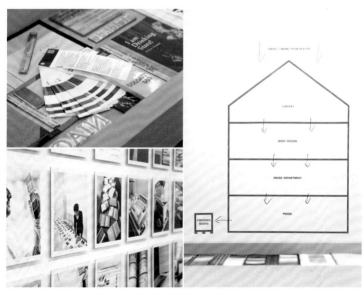

23 MAAD @Red Dot Design Museum

Map C, P.105

Helmed by the Red Dot Design Museum, this hyperlocal marketplace is more than a treasure trove of original finds. It is a community of creatives who crafts with anything from sewing machines to vintage cameras, and a test-bed for their artisan wares. Sift through a fashion student's handmade dresses, or be a budding tastemaker's guinea pig for her new ice-cream flavours and cold brew concoctions. Before you call it a night, volunteer as a model at Portraits After Dark, and take heart in knowing that you are fuelling the local arts scene in little ways.

🕐 1700-0000, one Friday each month
🏠 28 Maxwell Rd., 069120   ☎ +65 6534 7194
🔗 www.museum.red-dot.sg/maad
✏ Return slated for late 2017

"You can register to get your portrait drawn or take part as an artist at Portraits After Dark hosted by the Organisation of Illustrators Council (OIC)!"

– Esther Goh

24 Gillman Barracks

Map P, P.110

Before it became a contemporary arts enclave, the former British camp was built on a hill to fend off incoming troops from the sea. Anyone who has been to Gillman Barracks will tell you to visit in comfy shoes, but few know of the story behind its deserted location. Along the colonial corridors military men once trudged on, homegrown and international galleries bustle with happenings. If you are tired of the predictable TGIFs, Art After Dark – a bi-monthly outdoor party celebrating new exhibitions with food, music and hands-on installations – might be right up your alley.

🕐 Hours vary with galleries. Closed Mondays & P.H.
🏠 9 Lock Rd., 108937
🔗 www.gillmanbarracks.com
✐ Guided tours: weekly or monthly Fridays to Sundays at varied timings. Bookings required.

"Best to visit during open house events such as Art After Dark or Art Day Out which occurs once a month with outdoor events and pop-up stalls."

– Kelvin Lok, Couple

EXIT

Markets & Shops

Hipster streets, vintage thrift stores and lively pop-ups

Falling under the radar amidst the shopping malls are locales like Ann Siang and Haji Lane (#27), where all things hipster settle into curated boutiques and lifestyle stores. In the nearby Kampong Glam, The Heritage Shop (*93 Jln Sultan, 198997*) and Children Little Museum (*42 Bussorah St., 199460*) seem almost stuck in time, selling old-school memorabilia close to the hearts of Singaporeans.

Old souls will delight in the haphazard selection of typewriters and watch parts at Sungei Road Thieves Market, Singapore's last surviving flea market from the 1930s, although it's closing its final chapter in July 2017 to make way for new condos. The rummage continues at thrift stores like New2U (*96 Waterloo St., 187967*) and Lorgan's The Retro Store (*www.lorgans.com*), where the local TV station sources vintage furniture to assemble film sets for nostalgic dramas.

On a landmine of exciting pop-ups, creatives can be found peddling their crafts at Public Garden (*www.public-garden.com*) and The Local People (*thelocalpeoplesg.com*), while visitors have their portraits drawn by several artists simultaneously at the Market Of Artist And Designers (#23). Still, the luckiest are those who come just in time to soak up the Hari Raya festivities at Geylang Serai Ramadan Bazaar (#35).

Edwin Tan
Founder & creative director, Bravo

We make and shape brands that matter. We develop concepts bolder than Arial Bold and design with more finesse than Anna Wintour's hair. We love what we do.

Threadbare & Squirrel
P.055

Max Tan
Owner, MAX.TAN

I am the designer of my eponymous label, MAX.TAN. Much of my attention is paid to tailoring and draping while creating unexpected silhouettes and austere moods.

Colin Seah
Founder, Ministry of Design

I'm an architect. My wife and I run Ministry of Design, an architectural and interior design firm based in Singapore with offices in Kuala Lumpur and Beijing. We love calling Singapore home.

China Square Central
P.054

Haji Lane
P.056

Shing
Jewellery designer, Argentum

I am the creator behind Argentum, a jewellery label established in 1995. Trained in Central Saint Martins, I craft bodily adornments as expressions of the human condition.

BooksActually
P.059

Squelch Zines
Publisher

Made up of three Singaporean zine makers, Squelch Zines aims to promote the culture of self-publishing and self-expression through experimental crafts techniques.

Elyn Wong
Founder, Stolen

I am a creative director, installation artist, dreamer and designer behind ready-to-wear female apparel label Stolen. I love structured forms. I want to marry sexiness with structure.

Tong Mern Sern Antiques Arts & Crafts
P.058

Mustafa Centre
P.060

Zul Mahmod
Sound artist

I work at the forefront of Singapore's sound-media art. I am Singapore's first sound artist to have a full-on sound sculpture on show at the Singapore Pavilion of the 52nd Venice Biennale 2007.

Joo Chiat
P.062

Ricks Ang
Founder, Kitchen. Label

Ricks Ang is the creative force behind Singapore and Tokyo-based independent record label, Kitchen. Label, Ang is also a producer and part of ambient folk duo Aspidistrafly.

Stella Gwee
Co-founder, Shophouse & Co

At Shophouse & Co, we curate and create meaningful and memorable places. We are excited by stories, whether they are told through the space, culture or the community.

Tekka Market
P.061

Curated
Records
P.064

Yong
Owner, Somewhere Else

I run a small branding design studio called Somewhere Else. Easily bored and restless, I am always eager to find out what lies behind the paths that I do not take.

Geylang
Serai Market
P.066

Kane Tan & Sven Tan
Co-founders, In Good Company

We co-founded the ready-to-wear womenswear label with two friends in 2012. Our designs make for wardrobe essentials defined by a clean and modern aesthetic.

William Chan
Founder, TMRRW

I am a designer, artist and director. I am also the co-founder of art and design collective, PHUNK. I was named 'Designer of the Year' by President's Design Award in 2007.

Supermama
P.065

Basheer
Graphic
Books
P.067

25 China Square Central
Map C, P.105

The one-time living quarters of 'Samsui wom-en', the girls who came from China to labour in Singapore during the 1920s-1940s, have gained a new life as the headquarters of playthings. Its restaurants and bars are mainly filled with office workers, but toy collectors and window shoppers pour forth with different agendas, crowding collectible stores and weekend flea markets for unique finds. Spend your Sunday morning rummaging through Bandai and Marvel action figurines, antique homeware, and vintage knick-knacks like familiar Happy Meal toys aged gracefully from the 1990s.

🕒 Hours vary with shops
🏠 18 Cross St., 048423　📞 +65 6327 4473
🔳 www.chinasquarecentral.com
🔖 Flea market: 1100–1800 (Su)

"If you are a fellow toy, antique or craft collector, this is the place to be. You'll never know what priceless collectible you might be lucky enough to find."
– Edwin Tan, Bravo

26 Threadbare & Squirrel
Map K, P.109

For a break from predictable genres of retail therapy, indie establishments like Threadbare & Squirrel are your best bet. Shopping in the multi-label boutique is like browsing multiple walk-in wardrobes at once, each assembled with little regard for mainstream trends. Quality and uniqueness resonate across collections sourced from Singapore, Japan, Australia, Sweden, and Iceland, and these virtues peculiarly distinct in the fine threads by Gin Lee, the timeless cuts by Max Tan, and the theatricality of A.K.A Wayward.

🕑 1030–2130 daily
🏠 501 Orchard Rd., #02–20 Wheelock Pl., 238880
📞 +65 6235 0680
f Threadbare & Squirrel

"Not only can one find the most recent collection from MAX.TAN here in its full range but also discover other product designers as well."

– Max Tan, MAX.TAN

27 Haji Lane
Map I, P.108

Haji Lane is an exception in this sterile city where graffiti – from traditional Javanese murals to a painting of the beautiful Audrey Hepburn – is liberally splashed at every turn. It is home to a tight community of avant-garde designers and entrepreneurs, whose make-up is as eclectic as its palette. Hopping from one shophouse to another will take you from a barbershop (Hounds of Baskerville) inspired by Sherlock Holmes to a Scandinavian furniture shop-cum-café and bespoke bar. Along these bohemian-tuned streets, local online boutiques like Modparade and Vainglorious have also taken their first shots at brick-and-mortar stores.

🏠 Haji Ln., 189233

"*It's unpredictable because shops come and go but they are always surprising and authentic... and hip – from fashion to food to accessories.*"
– Colin Seah, Ministry of Design

28 Tong Mern Sern Antiques Arts & Crafts

Map C, P.105

The untrained eye will mistake this for a hoarder's cave, but what truly lies within is an unofficial museum of Singapore. Sprawled across the three-storey shophouse is a raw and arbitrary stockpile from *karung gunis* (rag-and-bone men) and vendors from the historic Thieves' Market which has been counting the days since 2014. Expect to light on treasures like industrial lamps and Kopitiam chairs as you scour the shop. Its star keepsake is a 100-year-old music box from Switzerland, painstakingly cared for by the shopkeeper to fight a winning battle against time.

🕐 0930–1730 (M–Sa), 1330– (Su)
🏠 51 Craig Rd., 089689
📞 +65 6223 1037 🔳 tmsantiques.com
🔗 Shop may be closed on public holidays

"Maybe I'm a fool but I'm a happy one, especially when I find my spoils. Go with an open mind. You never know what you could sniff out."

– Shing, Argentum

29 BooksActually
Map C, P.104

Paperback diehards will fall head over heels
for this indie bookstore. The quaint hideout in
Tiong Bahru is an interlude between cafés, and
you won't miss the potted plants and sketches
splashed across its storefront. Decked alongside
international bestsellers are local novelists and
poets, vintage bric-a-brac, and sensitive mate-
rial that has escaped the fate of censorship at
chain bookstores. Literature and authenticity
are at the heart of BooksActually, who plays
big brother to the community with regular
launches and readings in store.

🕐 1000–2000 (Tu–Sa), –1800 (Su–M)
🏠 9 Yong Siak St., 168645
📞 +65 6222 9195
URL www.booksactuallyshop.com

"You will be surprised by what their cats can do."
— Squelch Zines

30 Mustafa Centre
Map E, P.107

Singaporeans have a colloquial term "Bao Ga Liao" for "all-inclusive", and the legendary Mustafa Centre is the embodiment of just that. The mall opens 24/7 all year round, but you are better off visiting early in the morning to avoid crowds. Stocked with IT gadgets, electrical appliances, skincare, foodstuff and even gold, the variety is so massive, you stand a decent chance of surviving a zombie apocalypse here. Away from this chaotic but colourful labyrinth of bargains and cramped aisles, hit 'R' in the elevator to access Kebab's N Curries and fix your hunger pangs beneath a glass dome.

🕓 24hrs
🏠 145 Syed Alwi Rd., 207704
📞 +65 6295 5855
URL www.mustafa.com.sg

"The fact that it's open 24/7 makes it a super fun excursion for those who are suffering from jetlag. I come here when I need visual stimulation and crazy ideas."

– Elyn Wong, Stolen

31 Tekka Market
Map E, P.107

The soundtrack of Tekka Market mixes the
sharpening of choppers, opening of cockles,
scaling of fish and the occasional splash of
crushed ice. This multi-sensory grid is a parade
of everyday life, promising a wet market experience unparalleled by chain grocery stores. Start
the morning with Yakader's (#01-259) *dum biryani*, the steam-cooked version of *nasi biryani*,
at a hawker centre almost entirely dedicated to
Muslim and Indian food above the market. Climb
another flight of stairs and you will reach the
retail floor where you can find Chinese stallhold-
ers haggling amongst hand-embroidered saris
and scarves in fluent Tamil.

🕐 *0600 till late daily*
🏠 *665 Buffalo Rd., 210665*

*"The market has a life on its own and the stall owners
are friendly and very knowledgeable. There is one
shop that sells vegetables and plays jazz music."*

– Zul Mahmod

32 Joo Chiat
Map F, P 107

Basking in the old-world charm of Joo Chiat are designated safekeepers of Peranakan culture. In pre-war shophouses turned "home museums" like The Intan and Rumah Bebe, traditional Kebayas, beaded shoes and china-ware form only a subset of an extensive, lavish stash. Rise early on the weekend for Chin Mee Chin Confectionery (#44) or Kway Guan Huat's live popiah-making demo staged from 8.30am to 11am. Against a backdrop of heritage, the snazzier finds range from hipster cafés like Sinpopo to Rabbit Carrot Gun, a B&B where you can stay the night in a shophouse.

🏠 Joo Chiat
🔗 The Intan: the-intan.com; Rumah Bebe: rumahbebe.com; Kway Guan Huat: joochiatpopiah.com; Sinpopo: sinpopo.com; Rabbit Carrot Gun: www.rabbit-carrot-gun.com

"Stop by the row of beautiful shophouses along Koon Seng Road for a quick Instagram-worthy photo!"

– Stella Gwee, Shophouse & Co

33 Curated Records
Map C, P.104

In the age of Spotify, sifting through crates of records only happens when boy meets girl in Hollywood flicks. But at Curated Records, you can pick up a bite-sized piece of the 1980s for S$30-45 before the world went from analogue to digital. This hole-in-wall shop is an audiophile's dream come true, holding over 1000 vinyls from all the genres you can think of. If the library of mainstream and underground artistes – from Rihanna to Weezer – doesn't tickle your fancy, you can call dibs on new shipments or make special requests on their Facebook page.

🕐 1300–2000 (Tu–Su)
🏠 55 Tiong Bahru Rd., 160055
📞 +65 6438 3644
f Curated Records

"Store owner Tremon is always up for a chat. Feel free to ask for recommendations."

– Ricks Ang, Kitchen. Label

34 Supermama
Map I, P.108

Wooden benches and gravel flooring characterise just about the next minimalist store, but Supermama is far from typical. In a slew of pop-ups peddling the local identity in repetitive curios, it shuts the broken radio with sheer workmanship and a touch of traditional Japanese craft. In the signature Singapore Icons series, porcelain pieces are inspired by details of everyday life that often go unnoticed, like the timeless symmetry of HDB blocks. Another major hit is the Tabi socks designed to resemble childhood snacks that will still put a smile on every Singaporean's face.

🕐 1100–2000 daily
🏠 Flagship: 265 Beach Rd., 199544
📞 +65 6291 1946
🔗 www.supermama.sg

"A very active store with many self-initiated projects and events that have brought about unique art piece-like products."

– Yong, Somewhere Else

35 Geylang Serai Market
Map H, P.108

Like Tekka Market, this ethnic marketplace is a patchwork of sundries, snacks and clothes. Housewives are found jostling under its Minangkabau roof for spices that give their curries an extra kick, and freshly grated coconut to make traditional snack, *kueh*. Zealous exclamations of *Sedap!* – a Malay expression for 'yummy' – can be heard where hawkers tout an array of *nasi padang* and *goreng pisang*. Every *Hari Raya*, the Ramadan Bazaar will spoil you with newfangled treats like fried Oreos and rainbow bagels, alongside every Singaporean's night market staple – the almighty Ramly burger.

🕐 Wet market: 0630–1200 daily, Food centre: 0800–2200 daily
🏠 1 Geylang Serai, 402001
📞 +65 6589 8494

"*Visit in the run-up to Hari Raya. Food-wise, Hajjah Mona is an institution for nasi rames (mixed rice dish). Kambing soup and Indian rojak are also must-eats.*"
– Kane Tan & Sven Tan, In Good Company

36 Basheer Graphic Books

Map D, P.106

Checkered tiles and hardcovers stacked all the way to its rafters, Basheer Graphic Books is au fait with every design student in Singapore. The specialised bookstore sells imports from reputed art publishers, most of which are too niche to be found anywhere else. No matter your field in the creative industry, it is easy to lose track of time in a sea of titles on fashion design, architecture, copywriting, graphics, typography and more. Keep your eyes peeled for clearance goods from S$3, and weekly fairs in the complex peddling preloved reads and stationery.

🕐 1000-2000 (M-Sa), 1100-1830 (Su)
🏠 Bras Basah Complex #04-19, 231 Bain St., 180231
📞 +65 6336 0810
URL www.basheergraphic.com

"Have a chat with Mr. Nasser, the owner. He is by far the most knowledgeable person that I know on design trends and doesn't practise design as a profession."

– William Chan, TMRRW & PHUNK

Restaurants & Cafés

Veteran hawkers, themed cafés and novel dining concepts

Hainanese Chicken Rice and Laksa are the first order of business when a Singaporean returns from abroad. The local palate, big on strong flavours like *wok-hei* (the tang of piping hot wok) and chilli, has fueled the street food scene for decades at places like Lau Pa Sat (*18 Raffles Quay, 048582*) and Chinatown Complex (*335 Smith St., 050335*), where the world's cheapest Michelin-starred dish costs only S$2.

Café-hopping is a national hobby in Jalan Besar and Tiong Bahru, but even the most international of concept eateries are peppered with Singaporean touches that satiate a perennial obsession with hawker fare. There is nowhere else in the world where Chilli Crab Cheese Fries and Ondeh-Ondeh Pancakes will make sense.

Dining in Singapore is never a dull affair. Enjoy a romantic dinner in a restored chapel at The White Rabbit (*www.thewhiterabbit.com.sg*), or groove to local bands at a gastropark assembled entirely from shipping containers (*timbreplus.sg*). Better yet, catch your own dinner at a floating *kelong* called Smith Marine (*www.smithmarine. com.sg*), where you can enjoy a quiet sunset away from the hustle and bustle.

Edwin Low
Owner, Supermama

I am probably the most ordinary Singaporean you can find here – raised here, married and proudly own a three-room HDB flat. My shop is like a mom-and-pop store with a "designer" twist.

Kampong Glam Café
P.073

Kelly Lim aka kllylmrck
Visual artist

I started crocheting and knitting since I was seven. I create original, freeform sculptures that focus on texture and detail.

Pixin
Artist

I paint, draw, sew and make comics. When I am not making art, I cherish the time I spent with family and friends, where we wonder about our relationship to life under the same sky.

Redhill Market & Food Centre
P.072

Xiao Ya Tou
P.074

Yanda
Curator & designer

Under the name Do Not Design, Yanda creates art and dabbles in publishing and painting. He also blogs on theartistandhismodel. com, and co-produced CITIx60 Singapore.

Chye Seng Huat Hardware Coffee Bar
P.077

Leon Foo
Founder, Papa Palheta

I started the specialty coffee company in 2009. I actively travel to establish trade relationships with coffee farmers and co-operatives with quality and transparency of coffee in mind.

Bjorn Low
Co-founder, Edible Garden City

Trained in biodynamic agriculture, I run a rooftop farm on one of Singapore's busiest shopping streets. I believe that now is the time for people to reconnect with nature.

Looksee Looksee
P.076

Open Farm Community
P.078

miun
Artist

I express the norm in my own language. I work with varied mediums and enjoy living in Singapore, a place that inspires a new way of introspection into the modern world.

Chin Mee Chin Confectionery P.081

Jackson Tan
Artist, designer & curator

I'm the founding partner of PHUNK and the creative director of BLACK, specialising in branding, design and curation. I love collecting second hand vinyls, printing publications, football and film.

Tan Zi Xi aka MessyMsxi
Artist

MessyMsxi finds beauty in the vernacular. She pursued Illustration at Central Saint Martins with a DesignSingapore scholarship and now works on her own, full-time.

Brawn & Brains P.080

Por Kee Eating House P.082

New Ubin Seafood P.084

Wu Yanrong
Artist

Hi I'm Yanrong! I am a graphic designer and illustrator working mainly with watercolour. Most of my works are inspired by feelings, dreams and nature.

Olivia Lee
Industrial designer, OLIVIA LEE

OLIVIA LEE is an interdisciplinary studio straddling the worlds of art, design and experience. The studio communicates complex ideas simply, creating sensitive resonant work.

Grace Tan
Fashion designer

I began to work under the name kwodrent in 2003. My wearable works evolved into sculptural compositions and site-specific art installations, blurring the boundaries between disciplines.

East Coast Lagoon Food Village P.083

Yang Ji 194 & Good Beer Company P.085

37 Redhill Market & Food Centre
Map B, P.104

Google this hawker centre and Yan Fried Bee Hoon (#01-09) will show up on the first page. Its chicken wings may have shot to fame after the Prime Minister was spotted queuing for them, but there is more to Redhill Market & Food Centre than these crispy and juicy tenders. The volatile bits of Singapore's street food culture survive in this nondescript town. Machines and factories are slowly replacing kneading hands and nifty fingers, but vendors like Rong Xing Noodles And Xiao Long Bao (#01-65) and Fu Ming Carrot Cake (#01-49) still put up little shows of industrious handiwork.

🕑 Opening hours vary with store
🏠 85 Redhill Ln., 150085
🖋 Yan: 1500-2200 (Tu-Su);
Rong Xing: 1200-1400, 1700-2100 (W-M);
Fu Ming: 1500-0100 (M-W, F-Sa), 0600- (Su)

"From the healthy looking fried carrot cake, to the dessert uncle who dances to his techno beats serving sweet treats, Redhill is the go-to place for daily meals."
– Edwin Low, Supermama

38 Kampong Glam Café

Map I, P.108

You may be acquainted with *mee rebus* and *maggi goreng*, but these usual suspects form only a fraction of the full works you can find at Kampung Glam Café, where a smorgasbord of traditional Indonesian and Malay favourites is available till 2am daily. Specialties not often found in the regular coffeeshop include multiple varieties of *nasi goreng* and *roti kirai*, a noodle-like pancake eaten with a side of fragrant chicken curry. Seal the deal with a cup of Milo Dinosaur – a jazzed-up staple piled with undissolved Milo powder atop for twice the malty goodness.

🕐 0800–0200 daily
🏠 17 Bussorah St., 199438
📞 +65 6294 1697
🔗 kgglamcafe.ec-platform.net

"The café serves delicious and affordable Malay food. Do give yourself plenty of time to explore the quirky and colourful neighbourhood."

– Pixin

39 Xiao Ya Tou

Map C, P.105

As a throwback to Duxton's sketchy past of
brothels and opium dens in the 1850s, this
cheeky restaurant promises a visual feast of
oriental paraphernalia. Xiao Ya Tou's identity
is painted with lanterns, paper umbrellas and
pin-up girls, complete with patterned grilles
and retro tiles from the 1960s. Unabashedly
branded as 'naughty modern Asian cuisine',
its experimental nature is matched over the
stoves through the likes of Unagi Benedict
and Mentaiko Mac & Cheese. Mod-Sin hybrids
include Chai Tow Kway and Ovaltine Trifles, for
anyone who has ever wondered what upmar-
ket hawker fare would look like.

🕑 1000–2300 (M–Th), –0000 (F–Sa),
–1700 (Su)
🏠 6 Duxton Hill, 089592
📞 +65 6226 1965
URL www.xyt.sg

"*Coffee fanatics can have their revered cuppa with
the modern Asian cuisine, in a setting that brings
them back to Singapore in its old days.*"

– Kelly Lim aka kllylmrck

40 Looksee Looksee
Map I, P.108

Even if you're not a bookworm, this cute public room will convert you with an alluring combo of pastel washes, soft curves and natural lighting cast onto wood, leather and cane. Against a grid line background, banquette seats are scalloped to face a wall of hardcovers and paperbacks that come highly recommended by thought leaders in the creative and F&B scene, including personalities like Kenny Leck of BooksActually (P.032) and Bjorn Shen of Artichoke. Come spark your muse with a fresh read and specialty teas in cocktail- and coffee-inspired flavours, and return the gesture by tipping or buying the take-home merch.

🕙 1000-1800 (M-F), 1300-1700 (Sa)
🏠 267 Beach Rd., 199545 📞 +65 6338 8035
🔗 www.lobehold.com/looksee

"A gorgeous space that positively radiates creative energy. When you're done Instagram-ing every square inch of the interior, lose yourself in the books and tea."

– Yanda, Do Not Design

 ### 41 Chye Seng Huat Hardware Coffee Bar

Map E, P.107

Camouflaged in the industrial profiles of Tyrwhitt Road is a bogus hardware store, where you will find no trace of wire harnesses. Instead, it is a heavy-duty stop for *the* caffeine pilgrimage – a café, roastery, tasting room and retail section under one roof. The tribute to coffee goes as far as a dedicated island bar, where ordering a hand-pressed cup of joe treats you to its accompanying theatrics. Those who speak the language will delight in an extensive range of machines, accessories and their house roast to bring the good vibes back in take-home packs.

🕐 0900-2200 (Tu-Th & Su), -0000 (F-Sa)
📍 150 Tyrwhitt Rd., 207563
📞 +65 6396 0609 🔗 www.cshhcoffee.com

"If you take your coffee seriously, you must try the hand-brewed coffee served in locally handmade ceramics."

– Leon Foo, Papa Palheta

42 Open Farm Community
Map L, P.109

There is an ongoing joke that if you asked Singaporean kids where eggs come from, they will probably say 'supermarket'. In this land-scarce city, Open Farm Community is one of the rare few to champion a farm-to-table philosophy for local growers. The hilltop restaurant has a farm-garden in its backyard, so the herbs in your Rigatoni and Smashing Good Thyme cocktail are never harvested too far away. Save for wholesome meals, OFC also holds urban farming and culinary masterclasses, along with monthly social markets that sell artisan product like homemade jams and house plants.

🕐 Café: 0800-2100 daily, Restaurant: 1200-1600, 1800-2200 (M-F), 1100- (Sa-Su & P.H.)
🏠 130E Minden Rd., 248819 📞 +65 6264 7960
🔗 openfarmcommunity.com

"If you want to get your hands dirty and try growing your own food, OFC runs a community gardening session every week, free to attend by all."
– Bjorn Low, Edible Garden City

(43) Brawn & Brains

Map G, P.108

Within the spacious hideout, the medley of raw wood, cement and metal fits right into the industrial neighbourhood. Thanks to its full-length windows, the café basks in so much natural lighting that the communal tables feel almost like al fresco dining. The less-is-more mantra is also prevalent in its menu, unpretentious and well-loved with basics like earl grey pound cake and curried chicken wrap. Coffee, however, is the one thing Brawn & Brains fusses about. Take your pick between a rotating single origin or a chocolatey house blend of Ethiopian, Colombian and Brazilian beans.

🕐 0900-1900 (Tu-F), 0930- (Sa-Su & P.H.)
🏠 100 Guillemard Rd., #01-02, 399718
📞 +65 6348 0501 URL brawnandbrains.sg
🖉 Cash only

"They serve some of the best coffee in Singapore!"
– miun

44 Chin Mee Chin Confectionery
Map F, P.107

Along East Coast Road, a 1950s Hainanese coffeeshop is encapsulated in a time bubble made of powder blue walls and old-fashioned shutters. With a no-nonsense take on breakfast fare, Chin Mee Chin has escaped gentrification with a couple of chipped marble-tops and cracked mosaic tiles. Unlike the usual squares, their kaya toast takes the form of round, charcoal-grilled buns, with a luscious slab of butter plopped onto eggy coconut jam. Make sure you arrive early for their egg tarts, sugee cakes and luncheon meat rolls – they fly off the aluminium trays faster than you can say 'Kopi-C Siew Dai' (coffee with evaporated milk and less sugar).

🕐 0830–1600 (Tu–Su)
🏠 204 E Coast Rd., 428903
📞 +65 6345 0419
💳 Cash only

"Oldie but goodie! Go early for breakfast, order the half-boiled eggs, kaya toast with butter and kopi."

– Jackson Tan, BLACK & PHUNK

45 Por Kee Eating House
Map C, P.104

Por Kee has made headlines not only for hosting President Megawati of Indonesia, but also a public family squabble preceding its closure in 2013. Alas, the Cantonese *tze-char* restaurant (specialised in cooked and fried dishes) has since bounced back in full swing, tables still spilling over to adjacent carpark lots on busy evenings. From its choice of dinnerware to outdated platter decorations like flower-shaped biscuits, the heritage brand is unapologetically old-fashioned. Regulars wax lyrical about its glistening Champagne pork ribs and homemade bean curd, which has a crispy coat that when bitten into, gives way to a silky interior infused with *wok-hei*.

🕐 1130–1430, 1730–2330 daily 🏠 69 Seng Poh Ln., #01–02, 160069 📞 +65 6221 0582

"It's hard to find another watercress and pork rib soup that is as good as Por Kee's. Drips café down Tiong Poh Road opens late, hence a great place to chill after meal."

– Tan Zi Xi aka MessyMsxi

46 East Coast Lagoon Food Village

Map Q, P.110

The sands of East Coast Park are easily outshone by Sentosa's sparkling beaches, but in the department of seaside dining, nothing compares to a sprawling hawker centre with enough stalls to overwhelm both amateur tourists and expert Singaporean foodies. Identical specialties are offered across different vendors, but not all Hokkien *mee*, *tze-char* and satay are created equal. The general rule is to locate the longest queues or storefronts plastered with newspaper clippings. On a lucky day, you may even catch streetside hawkers roasting chestnuts and selling the ubiquitous ice-cream sandwich outside the centre.

🕐 1030-2300 daily
🏠 1220 East Coast Parkway, 468960

"Get barbecued seafood, hawker food, sugarcane juice, coconut water and beach in one place! Try to doggy-bag your food and eat by the sea."

– Wu Yanrong

47 New Ubin Seafood
Map R, P.111

It has been two decades since New Ubin moved from jetty shack to mainland Singapore, but the *tze-char* restaurant still retains its rustic *kampung*-style appearance and a ritual of using daily catch from the waters off Pulau Ubin. The US Angus rib-eye beef steak is one of its many experiments with American and European touches that has catapulted to bestseller status, served with claypot rice that had been fried with the meat's charred fat and burnt ends. Also noteworthy is the Garlic Baked Crab – an original that accentuates the crustacean's freshness with minimal seasoning.

🕐 1730–2200 (M), 1100–1430, 1730–2200 (Tu–Su & P.H.)
🏠 L6, Lam Soon Industrial Bldg., 63 Hillview Ave., 669569 📞 +65 6466 9558 🔗 ubinseafood.com

"Amidst auto parts and greasy garages, New Ubin shines like a diamond in the rough. Classics like 'heart attack fried rice' and meat platters are unmissable,"
– Olivia Lee

48 Yang Ji 194 & Good Beer Company

Map C, P.105

The Cantonese classic is not easy to pull off without a muddy taste, but Yang Ji 194 has nailed the Garlic Steamed Fish with 30 years of experience. Arrive well before dinnertime and S$18 gets you a tender fish head lathered with a savoury garlic sauce. You won't find a complementing white wine here, but Good Beer Company unlocks a whole new world of craft beer and hawker food pairings. The Taiwanese Lychee Beer, for example, cuts acidity well and is the designated partner-in-crime for your vinegar-laced bak chor mee.

🕐 1700–2200 daily
🏠 #02-57 Chinatown Complex Market, Blk. 335 Smith St., 050335

"My personal favourite is the non-spicy version of stir-fried kangkong (water spinach) – crunchy and juicy with unforgettable wok-hei!"

– Grace Tan, kwodrent

Nightlife

Stylish clubs, unconventional bars and laidback hangouts

By day, the CBD is efficient almost to a fault. But once dusk falls, it transforms into an arresting sight best taken from one of the world's tallest bars – 1-Altitude (*www.1-altitude.com*). Away from these swanky towers, Zouk (#60) regularly hosts the vivacious and K-Pop nights, while the indie flock to haunts like Refuge (*www.refuge.sg*), a shophouse turned American-style club lounge.

Discover a password-only hideout behind an innocuous bookshelf at The Library (*47 Keong Saik Rd., 089151*), or have your first-ever Kaya Toast cocktail or Bandung shot at bespoke bars like Bitters & Love (*www.bittersandlove.com*) and Hopscotch (*www.hopscotch. sg*). In the underground nightclub that is Cherry Discotheque (*FB: Cherry Discotheque Singapore*), old-school arcade games and a checkerboard dance floor will blast you back to the 1980s.

Away from the watering holes, there is plenty to kick back with if you're taking it easy. Get lost in the massive, 24-hour Mustafa Centre (#30) in Little India, or let the dingy back alleys of Swee Choon Tim Sum (*www.sweechoon.com*) transport you to an unusual sprawl of chaos and charm. Don't call it a night until you fall in love with roadside durian in Geylang – the country's infamous red light district.

Kevin Lim
Principal, Studio SKLIM

Architecturally trained, I provide bespoke solutions to the built environment. Born and bred in Singapore, I am enriched with working and living stints in London, Beijing and Tokyo.

Changi Village
Hawker
Centre
P.091

Selwyn Low
Co-founder, FARM

My name is Selwyn and I co-founded multidisciplinary studio FARM. I am trained in architecture, but my true interest lies in the intersection of space, objects and visuals.

Jerry Goh
Creative director, Hjgher

Hjgher specialises in design psychology. Together with editor Justin Long, I also created magazine *Underscore*. I believe design should be honest, timeless and above all, created for human.

Druggists
P.090

Maison
Ikkoku
Cocktail Bar
P.092

Chris Lee
Owner, Asylum

I am a father of a two-year-old so I had to hang my dancing shoes not so long ago. I am a designer by day and a glutton or alcoholic by night.

Ah Sam Cold
Drink Stall
P.094

Sofie Chandra
PR Director, Zouk

I'm fiercely loyal and passionate about good food and cocktails. I always seek out the best hidden gems during my travels. I'm also an occasional runner but prefer doing high intensity workouts.

André Chiang
Owner, Restaurant André

Celebrity chef Andre Chiang is noted for his unique approach to food, his "octo-philosophy". In 2015, the Best Restaurant in Singapore title went to Restaurant André.

28 Hong
Kong Street
P.093

D Bespoke
P.095

Wee Teng Wen
Founder, The Lo & Behold Group

An entrepreneur with a passion for innovation, Wee Teng Wen is behind some of Singapore's most notable bars and restaurants. His mission is to deliver original, timeless experiences.

Lee Tai Fu
P.098

Anonymous
Branding agency

Germaine Chong and Felix Ng form Anonymous. The multidisciplinary studio divides its time by half – 50% on designing for clients and the other 50% on studio projects.

Loof
P.096

Robert Zhao Renhui
Visual artist

I created The Institute of Critical Zoologists and The Land Archive. I work mainly with photography and explore human's relationship with the nature.

Cuscaden
Patio Cafe &
Pub
P.099

weish
Musician & teacher

I am an avid supporter of local theatre, art, and music. Not just for arts' own sake, but to spotlight those mind-blowing talents that are often left unnoticed in Singapore.

Lepark
P.102

Renyung
Co-founder, MATTER

Renyung is passionate about collaborations, co-creation and building enabling platforms. She co-founded MATTER, a socially motivated lifestyle label to connect artisans in Asia.

Jahan Loh
Artist

My roots are firmly entrenched in the polemics of both classical and street art, merging traditional mediums with guerilla aesthetics to forge a highly personal style.

Blu Jaz Cafe
P.100

Zouk
P.103

49 Druggists
Map E, P.107

Having inherited the facade of the Chinese Druggists Association, this bar is the stuff of fight scenes in Kung Fu movies. The repurposed pharmacist is accentuated with 70s-style mosaic tiles and latticed grilles, and since booze is a happy drug to some, its past life is hardly a dissonance. Behind a calligraphed plaque that reads "Tiger Leopard Hall", a sparkling row of custom-made taps dispenses craft beers from European breweries such as Thornbridge and Mikkeller. The bar grub, carrying Asian-style bites like Coffee Pork Ribs and Sichuan pickles, is also designed to complement each of the 23 brews available.

🕐 1600-0000 (Tu-Sa), 1400-2200 (Su)
🏠 119 Tyrwhitt Rd., 207547
📞 +65 6341 5967   f Druggists

"Ask the barkeeper for recommendations. Check out the beer paraphernalia that is used to house the water tap and sink near the toilet."

– Kevin Lim, Studio SKLIM

50 Changi Village Hawker Centre
Map O, P.110

Changi Village Hawker Centre is synonymous with *nasi lemak* (coconut rice), with multiple stalls each claiming to be the 'original'. Rookies can start with International Nasi Lemak (#01-57) and Mizzy's Corner (#01-26), but brace yourselves for queues even at non-peak timings. Many flock to the far-flung edge of Singapore for Mei Xiang's *goreng pisang* (banana tempura) and *cendol melaka* (pandan flavoured jelly and coconut milk), which earned its coveted authenticity by sourcing ingredients from Malacca. Cafés like Chock Full Of Beans are not too far away for a welcome respite from the tropical heat.

🕐 0600–0200 (M–Th), –0000 (F), 24hrs (Sa–Su)
🏠 2 Changi Village Rd., 500002
🔗 Chock Full of Beans: chockfullofbeans.com.sg

"This neighbourhood has an old world charm where everything seems to slow down."
– Selwyn Low, FARM

 51 Maison Ikkoku Cocktail Bar
Map I, P.108

Helmed by celebrity mixologist Ethan Leslie Leong, Maison Ikkoku sits on the uppermost storey of a three-in-one shophouse. Its al fresco rooftop is most glorious at the golden hour, when the sun sets over the majestic Masjid Sultan. In an industrial setting of white bricks and bare steel pipes, your wish – however minty, floral or strong – is the bartenders' command. Tricks in the bag include setting a stalk of rosemary aflame (MI2 Passionate Moment) and the frothing of milk in the MI White French Maid, a liqueur-based cocktail for coffee aficionados.

🕐 1800-0100 (Su-Th), -0200 (F-Sa & P.H. eve)
🏠 L2, 20 Kandahar St., 198885
📞 +65 6294 0078
f Maison Ikkoku

"You'd be in luck if mixologist Ethan is on duty. Tell him your current mood or craving and watch him perform his magic."

– Jerry Goh, Hjgh̲or

 ## 52 28 Hong Kong Street
Map C, P.105

Nothing spells hush-hush like nondescript doors, the absence of signage, and its haphazard attempt at a name. Your only foray into this Easter egg of a bar is through a dingy stairway, where you can follow the sound of hip hop classics past its shroud of mystery. Drinks are slightly steeper in the American-style hangout, unsurprising for top-grade cocktails with plenty of behind-the-scenes action: hand-chipped ice, organic herbs, and pineapple slices vacuum-sealed with coconut oil. The bestselling Truffle Mac & Cheese Balls also makes a neat prelude to your choice of technique-laden poison.

🕐 1800-0200 (Tu-Th), -0300 (F-Sa)
🏠 28 Hongkong St., 059667
📞 +65 6533 2001

"They serve the most wicked cocktails alongside a great vibe. Its location makes it easy to limp into a club when the tap runs dry. Their bar food is pretty awesome too."

– Chris Lee, Asylum

53 Ah Sam Cold Drink Stall
Map C, P.105

If you find yourself near a seedy looking massage parlour, you've got the right place. Its inconspicuous location is half its hipster quotient formulae, complete with black-and-gold sign boards and biscuit tins that have been unmistakably displaced from an old-world coffee shop. The bourbon-based Old Fashioned is one of its reinvented cocktails – a concoction now infused with Milo for an M18 rendition of the chocolate beverage. Should you feel peckish in between drinks, the bar is known for a neat Hokkien *mee* rivalling standards of its hawker counterparts.

🕐 1800–0000 (M-Th), –0300 (F-Sa)
🏠 60 Boat Quay, 049848
📞 +65 6535 0838
f Ah Sam Cold Drink Stall

"Amazingly well-balanced cocktails with local flavours. The food is yummy too. They have super addictive chips to munch on!"

– Sofie Chandra, Zouk

54 D Bespoke
Map C, P.105

Rarely do bespoke bars end up in a cross between British dapper and Japanese finesse, but Daiki Kanetaka's brainchild is one heck of a classy outlier. Immaculately clothed in suave leather and dark wood, this Ginza-style vault holds the tipples equivalent of fine-dining. Cocktails are meticulously paired with Kimura glassware, and ice is frozen with water that has been purified for four times, before being carved by special cleavers so it melts at a slower pace. The minimum spend of S$60 per pax, which may be a shocker at first, is justified by the sheer attention invested in its details.

🕙 1800-0100 (M-Th), -0200 (F-Sa), 1600-2300 (Su)
🏠 2 Bukit Pasoh Rd., 089816
📞 +65 8141 5741
🔗 dbespoke.sg

"If you are looking for a quiet, elegant place with cocktails of the highest quality without loud music, this is the place. Go smart casual."

– André Chiang, Restaurant André

55 Loof
Map D, P.106

Ditch the painful stilettos and swanky bars – after hours are meant for kicking back in comfort. As the underdog of the CBD, Loof defines this as beer pong, an eclectic mix of casual seating, and a garden rooftop against the panoramic skyline. There can be no guilt in sinful treats that are worth every calorie, and Loof's Chilli Crab Cheese Fries will have you nodding in agreement. Out of the quirky cocktails ranging from Stylo Milo to Kopi Cat, Little Pink Dot is perhaps the most photogenic - served in a light bulb with flowers and a skewered marshmallow.

🕐 1700–0100 (M–Th), –0200 (F–Sa)
🏠 331 North Bridge Rd.,
   #03–07 Odeon Towers Extension
   Rooftop, 188720
📞 +65 6337 9416
🔗 www.loof.com.sg

"Stop by The Mama Shop on your way out to pick some nostalgic gems and locally-inspired knick-knacks to round up the distinctive Singaporean experience."

– Wee Teng Wen, The Lo & Behold Group

56 Lee Tai Fu
Map A, P.104

Only at Lee Tai Fu can you glimpse into a complete stranger's horde without being intrusive. The Chiam Family has an astounding mass of typewriters, McDonald's Hello Kitty collectibles, and even *The Straits Times'* cover story on 30 January 1986 when NASA's Challenger space shuttle exploded. Like the make-up of its nostalgic reserves, an "anything goes" demeanour characterises a portfolio of fusion dishes and affordable craft beers. Order the Otah Pizza for a crowd-pleaser, and wash the umami notes down with a creamy stout by St. Peter's.

🕐 1500-2330 (Tu-Su)
🏠 16 Kim Tian Rd., 169251
📞 +65 6376 2338
URL www.leetaifu.asia

"Nice craft beers and the really nice owner make this a great place to chill after exploring Tiong Bahru."
– Robert Zhao Renhui

Cuscaden Patio Cafe & Pub

Map K, P.109

Few locals are familiar with Ming Arcade, but those who do keep the secret that is Cuscaden Patio Cafe & Bar. This low-key hideaway in the shadow of the booming Hard Rock Cafe has amassed a loyal following that almost single-handedly keeps the mall alive. There is no rush for the dwindling minutes of happy hour when cheap booze is available all the time. The signature chicken wings, fried to a robust crisp and paired with their homemade chilli sauce, are an imminent sequel to dinner that's impossible to resist.

🕐 1500-0100 (M, W-Th), -0200 (Tu), -0300 (F), 1600-0300 (Sa)
🏠 Ming Arcade, 21 Cuscaden Rd., #B1-111, 249720
📞 +65 6887 3319 f Cuscaden Patio Cafe & Pub

"Go for cheap beer, loud rock tunes and awesome fried chicken wings."
– Anonymous

58 Blu Jaz Cafe
Map I, P.108

By means of textile shops and Middle-Eastern eateries, Arab Street hems a non-native culture into one of Singapore's most laid back neighbourhoods. Fret not if you miss the colours and lights of Blu Jaz's Mediterranean-style storefront – it's a household name around that any vendor can direct you to. In the three-storey shophouse, bohemian vibes echo through a scatter of woven chairs and lounge seats that cosy up the place. Start your evening with a platter of Beef Shish Kebabs and Chicken Shawarma at the cafe, and call it a night only when the visiting DJs in the lounge do.

🕐 1200–0100 (M–Th), –0200 (F), 1500–0200 (Sa)
🏠 11 Bali Ln., 189848   ☎ +65 6292 3800
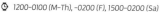 www.blujazcafe.net

"The entire area is full of my favourite spots, such as Teh Sarbat for authentic teh, the iconic Masjid Sultan, and the very quaint Museum of Independent Music."
– weish

59 Lepark
Map C, P.105

'Lepak' is a local slang for 'to loaf around', and you can do just that at this obscured bar after braving a maze of tour agencies and money changers to locate it. The grungy hideout sits on a rooftop carpark which hosts occasional live gigs, movie screenings and flea markets. Behind aluminium shutters, the compact laboratory invents Mod-Sin tapas like Poached Chicken Sushi – the locals' beloved Hainanese delicacy gone Japanese. When a jaw-dropping variety of over 80 craft beers presents the paradox of choice, the best of six words on a sample platter is the obvious answer.

🕐 1600-2300 (Tu-Th), -0000 (F), 1200-0000 (Sa), 1200-2300 (Su)
🏠 L6, People's Park Complex, 1 Park Rd., 059108
📞 +65 6908 5809 URL lepark.co

"This is also a getai venue where local and overseas bands and artistes take turns to perform. Good food, good party, good view...what more can we ask for?"
– Renying, MATTER

60 Zouk

Map C, P.105

The complex is a rite of passage that marks the coming-of-age in many Singaporeans' adolescence. In 2016, its wistful relocation to Clarke Quay brings with it a new restaurant and bar concept called Red Tail, serving fusion numbers like Scotch Century Egg and fries with Lup Cheong. Zouk has gotten a facelift after the move, and completing its neo-industrial aesthetics is a UFO-like structure that gives its underground vibes a cosmic touch. Having remained from its predecessor at Jiak Kim Street, Phuture is just a wall away with its discotheque theme and urban jam like hip-hop and R&B.

🕙 *2100–0300 (W & F), –0200 (Th), –0400 (Sa & P.H. eve)*
💲 *$25-45, Thursdays admit free*
🏠 *The Cannery, 3C River Valley Rd., 179022*
📞 *+65 6738 2988* 🔗 *zoukclub.com*
🎟 *18+, Strictly no slippers allowed*

"This is one of the oldest and most popular nightclubs in Singapore and Kuala Lumpur. Little knows that 'Zouk' is the French creole word for 'party'."

– Jahan Loh

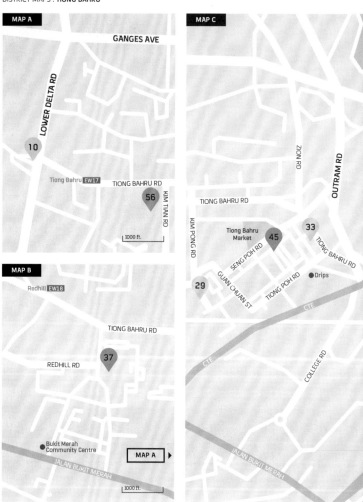

MAP A

GANGES AVE

LOWER DELTA RD

10

Tiong Bahru EW17 TIONG BAHRU RD

56

KIM TIAN RD

1000 ft.

MAP B

Redhill EW18

TIONG BAHRU RD

37

REDHILL RD

Bukit Merah
Community Centre

MAP A ▶

JALAN BUKIT MERAH

1000 ft.

MAP C

ZION RD

OUTRAM RD

TIONG BAHRU RD

KIM PONG RD

Tiong Bahru
Market

45

33

TIONG BAHRU RD

SENG POH RD

GUAN CHUAN ST

TIONG POH RD

●Drips

29

CTE

CTE

COLLEGE RD

JALAN BUKIT MERAH

- 2_PARKROYAL on Pickering
- 5_Pearl Bank Apartment
- 10_Tiong Bahru Estate
- 23_MAAD
  @Red Dot Design Museum
- 25_China Square Central
- 28_Tong Meng Sern Antiques
- 29_BooksActually
- 33_Curated Records

DISTRICT MAP : ROCHOR, ORCHARD, ALJUNIED, DOWNTOWN CORE

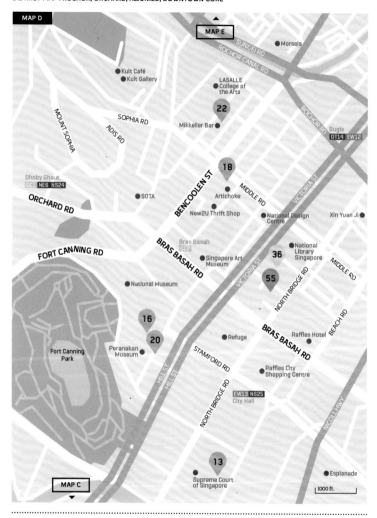

- 13_National Gallery Singapore
- 16_The Substation
- 18_Objectifs
- 20_Mulan Gallery
- 22_DECK
- 36_Basheer Graphic Books
- 55_Loof

MAP E

Kam Leng Hotel

49

41

LAVENDER ST

The Bao Makers
Café and Bakery

The
Refinery

HORNE RD

KITCHENER RD

SERANGOON RD

TYRWHITT RD

JLN BESAR

30

SYED ALWI RD

Scissors Cut
Curry Rice

RACE COURSE RD

KAMPONG KAPOR RD

Sri Veeramakaliamman
Temple

Swee Choon
Tim Sum
Restaurant

SERANGOON RD

JLN BESAR

JLN BERSEH

KALLANG RD

31

Sungei Road Laksa

EW11
Lavender

DT12 NE7
Little India

Madras New
Woodlands Restaurant

1000 ft.

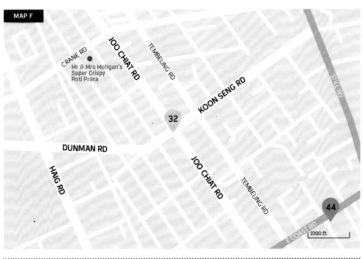

MAP F

CRANE RD

Mr & Mrs Mohgan's
Super Crispy
Roti Prata

JOO CHIAT RD

TEMBELING RD

KOON SENG RD

STILL RD

32

DUNMAN RD

JOO CHIAT RD

HAIG RD

TEMBELING RD

44

E COAST RD

1000 ft.

30_Mustafa Centre

31_Tekka Market

32_Joo Chiat

41_Chye Seng Huat
Hardware Coffee Bar

44_Chin Mee Chin
Confectionery

49_Druggists

DISTRICT MAPS : **ALJUNIED, KALLANG, ROCHOR**

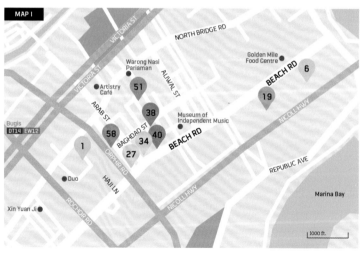

- 1_Parkview Square
- 6_Golden Mile Complex
- 19_The Projector
- 27_Haji Lane
- 34_Supermama
- 35_Geylang Serai Market
- 38_Kampong Glam Café
- 40_Looksee Looksee
- 43_Brawn & Brains
- 51_Maison Ikkoku Cocktail Bar
- 58_Blu Jaz

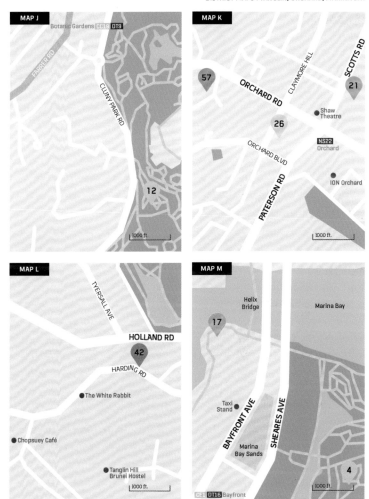

- 4_Gardens by the Bay
- 12_Singapore Botanic Gardens
- 17_ArtScience Museum
- 21_K+ Curatorial Space
- 26_Threadbare & Squirrel
- 42_Open Farm Community
- 57_Cuscaden Patio Cafe & Pub

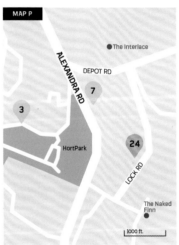

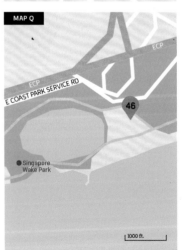

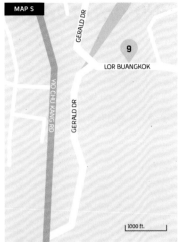

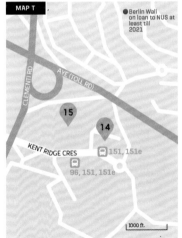

- 9_Kampong Lorong Buangkok
- 11_Blessed Sacrament Church
- 14_Lee Kong Chian Natural History Museum
- 15_NUS Museum
- 47_New Ubin Seafood

Accommodation

Hip hostels, boutique apartments & swanky hotels

No journey is perfect without a good night's sleep to recharge. Whether you're backpacking or on a business trip, our picks combine top quality and convenience, whatever your budget.

 $ < S$120   **$** S$121–200   **$** S$201+

The Club

Modernism and antiquity converge at this 19th-century colonial build. In a quiet location close to Chinatown, all 20 rooms are good value, with three interchange MRT stations nearby and plentiful top dining options in the hood to sate your appetite. Hotel guests will be treated to organic body products, premium bedding and delightful breakfast choices offered by one of its four restaurants and bars.

🏠 *28 Ann Siang Rd., 069708*
📞 *+65 6808 2188* **URL** *theclub.com.sg*   **$**

Naumi

Naumi exudes elegance within the heart of Singapore's Downtown Core. Guests can indulge in designer furniture from big names such as B&B Italia and Foscarini, or the seven-layer Egyptian cotton beddings. The hotel also boasts several fitness rooms, an infinity pool, and Indian cuisine in Table by Rang Mahal.

🏠 41 Seah St., 188396   📞 +65 6403 6000
URL www.naumihotel.com   Ⓢ

Lloyd's Inn

Following an extensive revamp, Lloyd's Inn reopens with naturally bright rooms. Decked with large windows looking out to lush greenery, all 34 rooms offer a restful stay in a clean, Zen style. Most rooms have a private garden or outdoor bathtubs to keep business travellers refreshed and rovers in.

🏠 2 Lloyd Rd., 239091
📞 +65 6737 7309 URL lloydsinn.com

Wanderlust Hotel

🏠 2 Dickson Rd., 209494
📞 +65 6396 3322
URL wanderlusthotel.com

💰

Adler Luxury Hostel

🏠 259 South Bridge Rd., 058808
📞 +65 6226 0173
URL www.adlerhostel.com

The Warehouse Hotel

🏠 320 Havelock Rd., 169628
📞 +65 6828 0000
URL www.thewarehousehotel.com

hôtel vagabond

🏠 39 Syed Alwi Rd., 207630
📞 +65 6291 6677
URL hotelvagabondsingapore.com

Notes

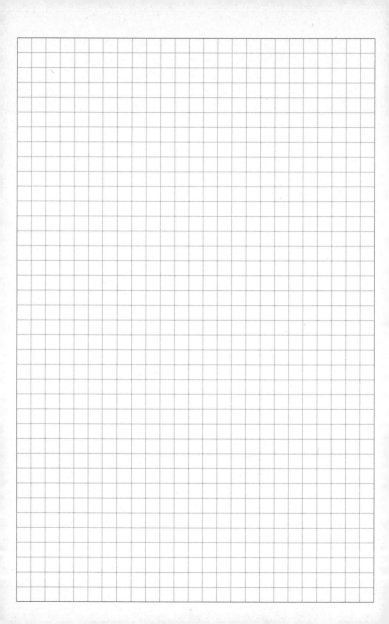

Index

Darius Ou, *P.014*
dariusou.work

Jackson Tan
@BLACK & PHUNK, *P.081*
blackdesign.com.sg
phunkstudio.com

Jonathan Yuen @Roots, *P.040*
whererootsare.com,
jonathanyuen.com

Kelvin Lok @Couple, *P.049*
couple.com.sg

Pann Lim @Kinetic, *P.028*
kinetic.com.sg, kplus.sg,
holycrap.sg, rubbishfamzine.com

Roy Wang Hang Yi
@Factory 1611, *P.034*
factory1611.com

Industrial

Edwin Low
@Supermama, *P.072*
supermama.sg

Melvin Ong @Desinere, *P.023*
desinere.com.sg

Olivia Lee, *P.084*
olivia-lee.com

Tiffany Loy, *P.036*
tiffanyloy.com

Multimedia

Zul Mahmod, *P.061*
zulmahmod.wordpress.com

William Chan
@TMRRW & PHUNK, *P.067*
tmrrw.com.sg

Music

Cherie Ko, *P.045*
@cherieko

Ricks Ang
@Kitchen.Label, *P.064*
kitchen-label.com

weish, *P.100*
FB: wweishh

Photography

Jovian Lim, *P.017*
jovianlim.com

Ernest Goh, *P.041*
ernestgoh.com

Publishing

Justin Zhuang
@In Plain Words, *P.038*
inplainwords.sg
Portrait by SAM & SAM

Kenny Leck
@BooksActually, *P.039*
booksactuallyshop.com

Squelch Zines, *P.059*
squelchzines.com

Photo & other credits

ArtScience Museum, *P.040*
(All) Marina Bay Sands

Brawn & Brains, *P.080*
(All) Marc Tan

DECK, *P.030, 046–047*
(All) Darren Soh

Gardens by the Bay, *P.017–019*
(All) Gardens by the Bay

Loof, *P.086, 096–97*
(All) Loof

MAAD @Red Dot Design
Museum, *P.048*
(All) Red Dot Design Museum
Singapore

NUS Museum, *P.038*
(All) NUS Museum

Objectifs, *P.041*
(All) Objectifs

The Projector, *P.042–43*
(All) Walter Navarro Peremarti

–
In Accommodation: all courtesy
of respective hotels.

CITIX60

CITIx60: Singapore

First published and distributed by
viction workshop ltd

viction:ary™

7C Seabright Plaza, 9-23 Shell Street,
North Point, Hong Kong

Url: www.victionary.com
Email: we@victionary.com
 @victionworkshop
 @victionary_
 @victionworkshop

Edited and produced by viction:ary

Concept & art direction: Victor Cheung
Research & editorial: Queenie Ho, Caroline Kong
Project coordination: Jovan Lip, Elisabeth Kwan, Katherine Wong
Design & map illustration: MW Wong, Frank Lo

Contributing coordinator & curator: Yanda
Contributing writer: Joyce Yang
Cover map illustration: Esther Goh
Count to 10 illustrations: Guillaume Kashima aka Funny Fun
Photography: Franz Navarrete

Content is compiled based on facts available as of March 2017. Travellers are
advised to check for updates from respective locations before your visit.

First edition
978-988-77148-0-4
Printed and bound in China

Acknowledgements

A special thank you to all creatives, photographer(s), editor, producers, com-
panies and organisations for your crucial contributions to our inspiration and
knowledge necessary for the creation of this book. And, to the many whose
names are not credited but have participated in the completion of the book,
we thank you for your input and continuous support all along.

CITIX60
City Guides

CITIx60 is a handpicked list of hot spots that illustrates the spirit of the world's most exhilarating design hubs. From what you see to where you stay, this city guide series leads you to experience the best — the places that only passionate insiders know and go.

Each volume is a unique collaboration with local creatives from selected cities. Known for their accomplishments in fields as varied as advertising, architecture and graphics, fashion, industry and food, music and publishing, these locals are at the cutting edge of what's on and when. Whether it's a one-day stopover or a longer trip, **CITIx60** is your inspirational guide.

Stay tuned for new editions.

City guides available now:

Amsterdam
Barcelona
Berlin
Copenhagen
Hong Kong
Istanbul
Lisbon
London
Los Angeles
Melbourne
Milan
New York
Paris
Portland
Singapore
Stockholm
Taipei
Tokyo
Vancouver
Vienna